50 Tokyo Table Dishes

By: Kelly Johnson

Table of Contents

- Soy-Glazed Chicken Donburi
- Miso Butter Ramen
- Tonkatsu with Cabbage Slaw
- Yuzu Shio Yakitori Skewers
- Tempura Udon Noodle Bowl
- Garlic Soybean Sprout Stir-Fry
- Spicy Tuna Onigiri
- Matcha Milk Pancakes
- Tokyo Street Yakisoba
- Creamy Uni Spaghetti
- Tofu Katsu Curry
- Sesame Soba with Scallions
- Negitoro Sushi Roll
- Karaage Chicken Bites
- Daikon and Pork Miso Soup
- Teriyaki Salmon Bento
- Tamago Sando (Egg Salad Sandwich)

- Curry Pan (Japanese Curry Bread)
- Shrimp and Avocado Temaki
- Kabocha Croquettes
- Chicken Nanban with Tartar Sauce
- Sweet Soy Glazed Eggplant (Nasu Dengaku)
- Tokyo-Style Okonomiyaki
- Shio Koji Marinated Grilled Fish
- Mochi Waffles with Black Sesame Syrup
- Gyuudon (Beef Bowl)
- Chashu Pork Buns
- Lotus Root Chips with Yuzu Salt
- Spinach Goma-ae (Sesame Dressing)
- Shoyu Ramen with Soft-Boiled Egg
- Eel Unagi Don
- Spicy Mentaiko Rice
- Ankake Tofu (Thick Sauce Tofu)
- Katsu Sando (Cutlet Sandwich)
- Hiyayakko (Chilled Tofu)
- Hijiki Seaweed Rice

- Wasabi-Mayo Grilled Squid
- Matcha Zenzai (Sweet Red Bean Dessert)
- Pickled Cucumber and Shiso Salad
- Japanese Potato Salad
- Butter Soy Corn Rice
- Omu Rice (Omelet Rice)
- Salmon Ochazuke (Tea-Poured Rice)
- Kinoko Itame (Mushroom Stir-Fry)
- Chicken Wings with Yuzu Kosho Glaze
- Mitarashi Dango (Sweet Soy Dumplings)
- Shiso Chicken Rolls
- Curry Udon
- Rice Ball Trio (Plum, Salmon, Kombu)
- Tokyo Milk Tea Pudding

Soy-Glazed Chicken Donburi

Ingredients:

- 2 boneless chicken thighs (skin-on preferred)
- Salt and pepper to taste
- 1 tbsp vegetable oil
- 2 tbsp soy sauce
- 1 tbsp mirin
- 1 tbsp sake
- 1 tbsp sugar
- 2 bowls cooked Japanese short-grain rice
- 1 soft-boiled egg, halved
- Sliced green onions, for garnish
- Toasted sesame seeds
- Pickled ginger (optional)

Instructions:

1. Season chicken with salt and pepper.
2. Heat oil in a skillet over medium-high heat. Place chicken skin-side down and sear until golden and crisp, about 5–6 minutes.
3. Flip and cook the other side for another 3–4 minutes.

4. Mix soy sauce, mirin, sake, and sugar in a small bowl. Add to the skillet and simmer for 2–3 minutes until thick and glossy.

5. Slice chicken and serve over hot rice with sauce spooned on top.

6. Garnish with green onions, sesame seeds, halved egg, and pickled ginger.

Miso Butter Ramen

Ingredients:

- 2 packs fresh or dried ramen noodles
- 3 cups chicken or vegetable broth
- 2 tbsp white miso paste
- 1 tbsp unsalted butter
- 1 garlic clove, minced
- 1 tsp soy sauce
- 1/2 tsp sesame oil
- 1/2 cup corn kernels (fresh or frozen)
- 1 soft-boiled egg, halved
- Sliced green onions and nori for topping

Instructions:

1. In a pot, heat butter over medium heat. Add garlic and sauté until fragrant.
2. Stir in miso paste, then slowly whisk in the broth to dissolve.
3. Add soy sauce and sesame oil. Simmer for 5 minutes.
4. In a separate pot, cook ramen noodles according to package directions. Drain.
5. Add corn to the broth and cook for another 2 minutes.
6. Divide noodles into bowls, pour broth over, and top with egg, green onions, and nori.

Tonkatsu with Cabbage Slaw

Ingredients:

- 2 pork loin cutlets
- Salt and pepper to taste
- 1/2 cup all-purpose flour
- 1 egg, beaten
- 1 cup panko breadcrumbs
- Oil for frying

Cabbage Slaw:

- 2 cups finely shredded cabbage
- 1 tbsp rice vinegar
- 1 tsp sugar
- 1/2 tsp salt

Tonkatsu Sauce:

- 2 tbsp Worcestershire sauce
- 1 tbsp ketchup
- 1 tsp soy sauce
- 1 tsp sugar

Instructions:

1. Season pork with salt and pepper. Dredge in flour, dip in egg, then coat in panko.

2. Heat oil in a skillet and fry cutlets until golden and crisp (about 3–4 minutes per side). Drain on paper towels.

3. Mix slaw ingredients in a bowl and let sit for 10 minutes.

4. Mix tonkatsu sauce ingredients in a small bowl.

5. Slice pork and serve with slaw and sauce on the side. Best with steamed rice.

Yuzu Shio Yakitori Skewers

Ingredients:

- 2 boneless chicken thighs, cut into bite-sized pieces
- 1 tbsp yuzu juice (or substitute lemon/lime juice)
- 1 tsp yuzu kosho (optional but authentic)
- 1 tbsp sake
- 1 tbsp salt
- 1/2 tsp sugar
- 1 tsp sesame oil
- Bamboo skewers, soaked in water

Instructions:

1. Combine yuzu juice, yuzu kosho, sake, salt, sugar, and sesame oil in a bowl.
2. Add chicken and marinate for at least 30 minutes.
3. Thread chicken onto skewers.
4. Grill over medium heat, turning frequently until cooked through and lightly charred, about 8–10 minutes.
5. Serve with a sprinkle of salt or a squeeze of yuzu/lemon.

Tempura Udon Noodle Bowl

Ingredients:

- 2 portions udon noodles (fresh or frozen)
- 4–6 pieces assorted vegetable and shrimp tempura (store-bought or homemade)
- 3 cups dashi broth
- 2 tbsp soy sauce
- 1 tbsp mirin
- 1 tsp sugar
- Sliced green onions
- Kamaboko (fish cake), optional

Instructions:

1. In a pot, bring dashi, soy sauce, mirin, and sugar to a simmer.
2. Cook udon noodles according to package instructions, then drain.
3. Divide noodles into bowls and pour hot broth over.
4. Top with tempura, green onions, and kamaboko slices if using. Serve hot.

Garlic Soybean Sprout Stir-Fry

Ingredients:

- 3 cups soybean sprouts (moyashi)
- 1 tbsp sesame oil
- 2 garlic cloves, thinly sliced
- 1 tbsp soy sauce
- 1/2 tsp salt
- 1 tsp toasted sesame seeds

Instructions:

1. Heat sesame oil in a pan over medium heat. Add garlic and cook until fragrant.
2. Add soybean sprouts and stir-fry for 2–3 minutes until slightly wilted but still crisp.
3. Add soy sauce and salt, toss to coat.
4. Sprinkle with sesame seeds and serve as a side dish or over rice.

Spicy Tuna Onigiri

Ingredients:

- 2 cups cooked Japanese rice
- 1 can tuna, drained
- 1 tbsp mayonnaise
- 1 tsp sriracha or gochujang
- Salt, to taste
- 2 sheets nori, cut into strips

Instructions:

1. Mix tuna, mayo, and sriracha in a bowl.
2. With wet hands, take a small handful of rice, flatten slightly, and add 1 tsp of spicy tuna mix in the center.
3. Enclose the filling and shape into a triangle.
4. Wrap with a strip of nori and serve.

Matcha Milk Pancakes

Ingredients:

- 1 cup all-purpose flour
- 1 tbsp matcha powder
- 1 tbsp sugar
- 1 tsp baking powder
- 1/2 cup milk
- 1 egg
- 1 tbsp melted butter
- Sweetened condensed milk or whipped cream, for topping

Instructions:

1. In a bowl, mix flour, matcha, sugar, and baking powder.
2. In another bowl, whisk egg, milk, and butter. Combine with dry ingredients.
3. Cook pancakes on a lightly greased pan over medium heat until bubbles form and edges set, then flip.
4. Stack and drizzle with condensed milk or top with whipped cream.

Tokyo Street Yakisoba

Ingredients:

- 2 packs yakisoba noodles
- 1/2 cup sliced pork belly or chicken
- 1/2 cup sliced cabbage
- 1/4 cup julienned carrots
- 1/4 cup sliced onion
- 2 tbsp yakisoba sauce (or mix Worcestershire sauce, ketchup, and soy sauce)
- Pickled red ginger and aonori (seaweed flakes) for garnish

Instructions:

1. Heat oil in a skillet. Stir-fry meat until browned.
2. Add vegetables and cook until just tender.
3. Add noodles and pour sauce over. Toss everything together and stir-fry until hot.
4. Garnish with red ginger and aonori.

Creamy Uni Spaghetti

Ingredients:

- 200g spaghetti
- 100g fresh or thawed uni (sea urchin)
- 1 tbsp butter
- 1/4 cup heavy cream
- 1 tbsp soy sauce
- 1 clove garlic, minced
- Chopped chives or shredded nori, for garnish

Instructions:

1. Cook spaghetti until al dente. Drain, reserving 1/4 cup pasta water.
2. In a pan, melt butter and sauté garlic until fragrant.
3. Add cream and soy sauce, then stir in uni (reserve a little for garnish).
4. Toss in pasta and mix until coated. Add pasta water if needed.
5. Serve topped with uni, chives, or nori.

Tofu Katsu Curry

Ingredients:

- 1 block firm tofu, pressed and sliced
- Salt and pepper
- 1/4 cup flour
- 1 egg, beaten
- 1 cup panko breadcrumbs
- Oil for frying

Curry Sauce:

- 1/2 onion, sliced
- 1 carrot, chopped
- 1 potato, chopped
- 2 cups water
- 1/2 block Japanese curry roux

Instructions:

1. Coat tofu slices in flour, egg, and panko.
2. Fry until golden and crispy. Set aside.
3. In a pot, simmer onion, carrot, and potato in water until soft.
4. Add curry roux and stir until thickened.

5. Serve curry over rice with tofu katsu on top.

Sesame Soba with Scallions

Ingredients:

- 2 bundles soba noodles
- 2 tbsp soy sauce
- 1 tbsp rice vinegar
- 1 tbsp sesame oil
- 1 tsp sugar
- 1 tbsp toasted sesame seeds
- 2 stalks scallions, finely sliced

Instructions:

1. Cook soba noodles, rinse under cold water, and drain.
2. Mix soy sauce, vinegar, sesame oil, and sugar in a bowl.
3. Toss noodles with sauce, sesame seeds, and scallions.
4. Serve chilled or at room temperature.

Negitoro Sushi Roll

Ingredients:

- 1 cup sushi rice, cooked and seasoned
- 100g fatty tuna (toro), minced
- 1 green onion, finely chopped
- 2 sheets nori
- Wasabi and soy sauce, to serve

Instructions:

1. Mix minced tuna with green onion.
2. Place nori on a sushi mat, spread rice thinly, leaving an edge at the top.
3. Add negitoro filling in a line.
4. Roll tightly, then slice into 6–8 pieces.
5. Serve with wasabi and soy sauce.

Karaage Chicken Bites

Ingredients:

- 2 chicken thighs, cut into bite-size pieces
- 1 tbsp soy sauce
- 1 tbsp sake
- 1 tsp grated ginger
- 1 tsp garlic, minced
- 1/2 cup potato starch or cornstarch
- Oil for frying
- Lemon wedges, optional

Instructions:

1. Marinate chicken in soy sauce, sake, ginger, and garlic for 15–30 minutes.
2. Dredge chicken in potato starch.
3. Fry in hot oil until golden and crispy, about 4–5 minutes.
4. Drain and serve with lemon wedges.

Daikon and Pork Miso Soup

Ingredients:

- 150g thinly sliced pork belly
- 1/2 daikon radish, peeled and thinly sliced
- 1/4 onion, sliced
- 3 cups dashi broth
- 2 tbsp miso paste
- 1 tbsp soy sauce
- 1 tsp sesame oil
- Chopped scallions, for garnish

Instructions:

1. Heat sesame oil in a pot and sauté pork until just cooked.
2. Add daikon and onion; stir briefly.
3. Pour in dashi and bring to a simmer. Cook until daikon is tender.
4. Reduce heat and dissolve miso paste in a ladleful of hot broth before mixing in.
5. Add soy sauce, stir, and serve garnished with scallions.

Teriyaki Salmon Bento

Ingredients:

- 2 salmon fillets
- 2 tbsp soy sauce
- 1 tbsp mirin
- 1 tbsp sake
- 1 tbsp sugar
- Steamed rice
- Blanched broccoli or pickled vegetables for side

Instructions:

1. Combine soy sauce, mirin, sake, and sugar in a pan; simmer to thicken slightly.
2. Add salmon fillets and cook over medium heat, basting until glazed.
3. Pack into a bento box with steamed rice and vegetables.

Tamago Sando (Egg Salad Sandwich)

Ingredients:

- 3 eggs
- 2 tbsp Japanese mayo
- Salt and pepper
- 2 slices soft white milk bread
- Butter, optional

Instructions:

1. Boil eggs for 10 minutes. Cool, peel, and mash.
2. Mix with mayo, salt, and pepper.
3. Butter bread slices if desired. Spread egg salad evenly and sandwich together.
4. Trim crusts and cut in half before serving.

Curry Pan (Japanese Curry Bread)

Ingredients:

- Japanese curry filling (cooled and thick)
- Bread dough (store-bought or homemade)
- 1 egg, beaten
- Panko breadcrumbs
- Oil for deep frying

Instructions:

1. Divide dough into balls, flatten, and place a spoonful of curry inside.
2. Seal and shape into an oval. Dip in beaten egg and coat with panko.
3. Deep fry until golden and crisp. Drain on paper towels and serve warm.

Shrimp and Avocado Temaki

Ingredients:

- 1 cup sushi rice, seasoned
- 6 nori squares
- 6 cooked shrimp, sliced lengthwise
- 1/2 avocado, sliced
- Wasabi and soy sauce, to serve

Instructions:

1. Place a spoonful of rice diagonally on one corner of nori.
2. Top with shrimp and avocado.
3. Roll into a cone shape. Serve immediately with wasabi and soy sauce.

Kabocha Croquettes

Ingredients:

- 1/2 kabocha squash, steamed and mashed
- 1/4 onion, finely diced and sautéed
- Salt and pepper
- Flour, egg, and panko for breading
- Oil for frying

Instructions:

1. Mix mashed kabocha with onion, salt, and pepper.
2. Shape into small patties. Coat in flour, egg, and panko.
3. Fry until golden. Drain and serve with tonkatsu sauce.

Chicken Nanban with Tartar Sauce

Ingredients:

- 2 chicken thighs, boneless
- Salt, pepper, and flour
- 1 egg, beaten
- Oil for frying

Nanban Sauce:

- 2 tbsp soy sauce
- 2 tbsp rice vinegar
- 1 tbsp sugar

Tartar Sauce:

- 1 boiled egg, chopped
- 2 tbsp mayo
- 1 tbsp chopped pickles or onions

Instructions:

1. Season chicken, coat with flour and egg, then fry until golden.
2. Simmer nanban sauce and pour over freshly fried chicken.
3. Serve with tartar sauce on top or on the side.

Sweet Soy Glazed Eggplant (Nasu Dengaku)

Ingredients:

- 2 small eggplants, halved
- 1 tbsp sesame oil

Glaze:

- 1 tbsp miso
- 1 tbsp mirin
- 1 tbsp sugar
- 1 tsp soy sauce

Instructions:

1. Score eggplant flesh and pan-fry cut side down in sesame oil until tender.
2. Mix glaze ingredients and brush over eggplant.
3. Broil or bake until caramelized. Serve warm.

Tokyo-Style Okonomiyaki

Ingredients:

- 1 cup flour
- 2/3 cup dashi or water
- 1 egg
- 1/2 cup chopped cabbage
- 2 tbsp green onions
- Sliced pork belly (optional)

Toppings:

- Okonomiyaki sauce
- Japanese mayo
- Bonito flakes
- Aonori (seaweed flakes)

Instructions:

1. Mix flour, dashi, and egg into a batter. Fold in cabbage and onions.
2. Pour into a hot greased skillet and top with pork slices.
3. Cook until set, flip, and finish cooking.
4. Drizzle with sauces and top with bonito flakes and aonori.

Shio Koji Marinated Grilled Fish

Ingredients:

- 2 fillets of white fish (like cod or mackerel)
- 2 tbsp shio koji

Instructions:

1. Rub fish with shio koji and refrigerate for 4–6 hours.
2. Wipe off excess marinade and grill or pan-fry until golden and cooked through.
3. Serve with rice and pickles.

Mochi Waffles with Black Sesame Syrup

Ingredients:

- 1 cup mochiko (sweet rice flour)
- 1/2 cup milk
- 1/4 cup sugar
- 1 egg
- 1/2 tsp baking powder

Black Sesame Syrup:

- 2 tbsp black sesame paste
- 2 tbsp honey or maple syrup

Instructions:

1. Whisk mochiko, sugar, baking powder, milk, and egg into a smooth batter.
2. Cook in a waffle iron until crisp.
3. Mix sesame paste and honey to make syrup. Drizzle over waffles and serve warm.

Gyuudon (Beef Bowl)

Ingredients:

- 300g thinly sliced beef (preferably ribeye or sirloin)
- 1/2 onion, thinly sliced
- 2 tbsp soy sauce
- 1 tbsp mirin
- 1 tbsp sake
- 1 tbsp sugar
- 2 cups dashi broth
- Steamed rice
- Pickled ginger, for garnish

Instructions:

1. In a pan, sauté onions until translucent.
2. Add beef and cook until browned.
3. Pour in soy sauce, mirin, sake, sugar, and dashi. Simmer for 5 minutes.
4. Serve the beef and sauce over steamed rice and garnish with pickled ginger.

Chashu Pork Buns

Ingredients:

- 500g pork belly, rolled and tied
- 2 tbsp soy sauce
- 1 tbsp sake
- 1 tbsp mirin
- 1 tbsp sugar
- 2 cups water
- Steamed bao buns

Instructions:

1. Simmer pork belly in soy sauce, sake, mirin, sugar, and water for 2-3 hours until tender.
2. Slice pork and place in steamed bao buns.
3. Serve with your choice of condiments (scallions, pickles, or mustard).

Lotus Root Chips with Yuzu Salt

Ingredients:

- 1 lotus root, thinly sliced
- 1 cup vegetable oil for frying
- 1 tsp yuzu kosho or yuzu zest
- Salt, to taste

Instructions:

1. Heat oil in a pan to 350°F (175°C). Fry lotus root slices until crispy and golden.
2. Drain on paper towels and season with salt and yuzu zest or yuzu kosho.
3. Serve as a crispy snack or appetizer.

Spinach Goma-ae (Sesame Dressing)

Ingredients:

- 200g spinach, blanched
- 2 tbsp sesame seeds
- 1 tbsp soy sauce
- 1 tbsp sugar
- 1 tsp mirin

Instructions:

1. Toast sesame seeds in a dry pan and grind them into a fine paste.
2. Mix the sesame paste with soy sauce, sugar, and mirin.
3. Toss the spinach in the sesame dressing and serve chilled.

Shoyu Ramen with Soft-Boiled Egg

Ingredients:

- 2 portions ramen noodles
- 4 cups chicken broth
- 2 tbsp soy sauce
- 1 tbsp mirin
- 1/2 tbsp miso paste
- 2 soft-boiled eggs
- Green onions, sliced
- Nori, for garnish

Instructions:

1. Cook ramen noodles according to package instructions and set aside.
2. Simmer chicken broth with soy sauce, mirin, and miso paste.
3. Place noodles in bowls, pour hot broth over, and top with soft-boiled eggs, green onions, and nori.

Eel Unagi Don

Ingredients:

- 2 fillets grilled eel (unagi)
- 2 cups steamed rice
- 2 tbsp unagi sauce (or eel sauce)
- Pickled ginger, for garnish

Instructions:

1. Heat eel fillets and drizzle with unagi sauce.
2. Serve eel over steamed rice and garnish with pickled ginger.

Spicy Mentaiko Rice

Ingredients:

- 2 cups steamed rice
- 100g mentaiko (spicy cod roe)
- 1 tbsp mayonnaise
- 1 tbsp soy sauce
- 1 tsp sesame oil

Instructions:

1. Mix mentaiko, mayonnaise, soy sauce, and sesame oil.
2. Serve over hot rice and toss to combine.
3. Garnish with chopped nori and sesame seeds.

Ankake Tofu (Thick Sauce Tofu)

Ingredients:

- 1 block silken tofu
- 1 tbsp soy sauce
- 1 tbsp sake
- 1 tbsp cornstarch mixed with 2 tbsp water
- 1 tbsp sesame oil
- 2 tsp sugar
- 1 green onion, chopped

Instructions:

1. Sauté tofu in sesame oil until golden on both sides.
2. Mix soy sauce, sake, sugar, and cornstarch slurry in a bowl. Add to the pan.
3. Stir until the sauce thickens and coats the tofu. Garnish with chopped green onion.

Katsu Sando (Cutlet Sandwich)

Ingredients:

- 2 pieces of tonkatsu (fried pork cutlet)
- 4 slices soft white bread
- Japanese mayonnaise
- Tonkatsu sauce

Instructions:

1. Spread mayonnaise and tonkatsu sauce on bread slices.
2. Place fried tonkatsu between slices of bread.
3. Cut into halves or quarters and serve immediately.

Hiyayakko (Chilled Tofu)

Ingredients:

- 1 block silken tofu
- 1 tbsp soy sauce
- 1 tsp sesame oil
- Chopped scallions
- Grated ginger
- Bonito flakes, for garnish

Instructions:

1. Chill the tofu in the refrigerator for an hour.
2. Drizzle with soy sauce and sesame oil.
3. Top with scallions, grated ginger, and bonito flakes before serving.

Hijiki Seaweed Rice

Ingredients:

- 2 tbsp dried hijiki seaweed
- 2 cups steamed rice
- 1 tbsp soy sauce
- 1 tsp sugar
- 1 tbsp sesame oil

Instructions:

1. Rehydrate hijiki seaweed in warm water for 10 minutes.
2. Stir-fry hijiki in sesame oil with soy sauce and sugar.
3. Mix into steamed rice and serve warm.

Wasabi-Mayo Grilled Squid

Ingredients:

- 2 whole squid, cleaned and scored
- 2 tbsp mayonnaise
- 1 tsp wasabi paste
- 1 tbsp soy sauce
- 1 tsp sesame oil
- Lemon wedges, for serving

Instructions:

1. Mix mayonnaise, wasabi, soy sauce, and sesame oil to make a marinade.
2. Coat the squid in the marinade and let sit for 10–15 minutes.
3. Grill squid on medium heat for about 3–4 minutes on each side, until charred and cooked through.
4. Serve with lemon wedges.

Matcha Zenzai (Sweet Red Bean Dessert)

Ingredients:

- 1/2 cup sweet red beans (azuki beans), cooked and mashed
- 1 tbsp matcha powder
- 1 cup dango (mochi balls) or shiratama flour balls
- 2 tbsp sugar
- 1/2 cup water
- 1 tbsp red bean paste (optional for topping)

Instructions:

1. In a saucepan, combine red beans, matcha powder, sugar, and water. Simmer over low heat until smooth.
2. Cook dango or mochi balls according to package instructions.
3. Serve warm in bowls, adding the matcha red bean mixture over the mochi balls.
4. Optionally top with a spoonful of red bean paste.

Pickled Cucumber and Shiso Salad

Ingredients:

- 1 cucumber, thinly sliced
- 6 shiso leaves, shredded
- 2 tbsp rice vinegar
- 1 tsp sugar
- 1 tsp soy sauce
- Pinch of salt
- Sesame seeds, for garnish

Instructions:

1. Mix rice vinegar, sugar, soy sauce, and salt in a bowl until the sugar dissolves.
2. Toss cucumber slices and shredded shiso in the dressing.
3. Let sit for 10 minutes before serving.
4. Garnish with sesame seeds.

Japanese Potato Salad

Ingredients:

- 4 medium potatoes, peeled and boiled
- 1/2 cucumber, thinly sliced
- 2 tbsp grated carrot
- 2 tbsp mayonnaise
- 1 tbsp rice vinegar
- 1 tsp mustard
- Salt and pepper, to taste

Instructions:

1. Mash the boiled potatoes and let cool slightly.
2. Add cucumber, grated carrot, mayonnaise, rice vinegar, and mustard. Mix well.
3. Season with salt and pepper and refrigerate for 30 minutes before serving.

Butter Soy Corn Rice

Ingredients:

- 2 cups steamed rice
- 1 cup corn kernels (fresh or frozen)
- 1 tbsp butter
- 1 tbsp soy sauce
- Chopped green onions, for garnish

Instructions:

1. In a pan, sauté corn in butter until heated through.
2. Add soy sauce and stir well.
3. Mix the buttered corn with steamed rice.
4. Garnish with chopped green onions before serving.

Omu Rice (Omelet Rice)

Ingredients:

- 2 eggs
- 1/2 cup cooked rice (preferably day-old rice)
- 2 tbsp ketchup
- 1 tbsp soy sauce
- 1 tbsp butter
- 1/4 onion, chopped
- 1/2 cup cooked chicken or ham (optional)

Instructions:

1. In a pan, sauté onion in butter until softened, then add rice and stir-fry for 2–3 minutes.
2. Add ketchup and soy sauce, mixing well.
3. In a separate pan, whisk eggs and cook in butter until soft and slightly runny.
4. Place the rice mixture in the center of the omelet and fold the sides over. Serve immediately.

Salmon Ochazuke (Tea-Poured Rice)

Ingredients:

- 2 salmon fillets, grilled or pan-fried
- 2 cups steamed rice
- 2 cups hot green tea (or dashi broth)
- 1 tbsp soy sauce
- Pickled plum (umeboshi), for garnish
- Nori strips, for garnish

Instructions:

1. Flake the cooked salmon over steamed rice.
2. Pour hot green tea (or dashi) over the rice and salmon.
3. Drizzle with soy sauce and garnish with pickled plum and nori strips.

Kinoko Itame (Mushroom Stir-Fry)

Ingredients:

- 200g mixed mushrooms (shiitake, enoki, oyster), sliced
- 1 tbsp soy sauce
- 1 tsp sesame oil
- 1 tsp mirin
- 2 cloves garlic, minced
- 1 tbsp chopped green onions

Instructions:

1. Heat sesame oil in a pan and sauté garlic until fragrant.
2. Add mushrooms and stir-fry until tender, about 5–6 minutes.
3. Add soy sauce and mirin, stir to combine, and cook for another 2 minutes.
4. Garnish with green onions and serve warm.

Chicken Wings with Yuzu Kosho Glaze

Ingredients:

- 10 chicken wings, separated into drumettes and flats
- 2 tbsp soy sauce
- 1 tbsp honey
- 1 tbsp yuzu kosho
- 1 tbsp sesame oil
- 1 tsp rice vinegar
- Sesame seeds, for garnish
- Chopped green onions, for garnish

Instructions:

1. Preheat the oven to 400°F (200°C).
2. In a bowl, mix soy sauce, honey, yuzu kosho, sesame oil, and rice vinegar.
3. Toss the chicken wings in the glaze mixture and spread them on a baking sheet.
4. Bake for 20–25 minutes, flipping halfway through, until crispy and golden.
5. Garnish with sesame seeds and chopped green onions before serving.

Mitarashi Dango (Sweet Soy Dumplings)

Ingredients:

- 1 cup mochiko (glutinous rice flour)
- 2/3 cup water
- 2 tbsp sugar
- 2 tbsp soy sauce
- 1 tbsp mirin
- 1 tbsp corn syrup
- Bamboo skewers

Instructions:

1. Mix mochiko and water until smooth. Roll the dough into small balls and thread them onto bamboo skewers.
2. Boil the skewered dumplings in water for about 5 minutes until they float.
3. Mix soy sauce, mirin, sugar, and corn syrup in a pan. Bring to a simmer to form a glaze.
4. Brush the glaze over the cooked dango and serve warm.

Shiso Chicken Rolls

Ingredients:

- 2 chicken breasts, thinly sliced
- 12 shiso leaves
- 2 tbsp soy sauce
- 1 tbsp mirin
- 1 tsp sesame oil
- 1 tsp grated ginger

Instructions:

1. Lay a shiso leaf on each chicken slice and roll them up tightly.
2. Heat sesame oil in a pan and sauté the chicken rolls until cooked through, about 6-8 minutes.
3. Mix soy sauce, mirin, and ginger in a bowl and pour over the rolls.
4. Serve warm, garnished with extra shiso leaves.

Curry Udon

Ingredients:

- 2 portions udon noodles
- 1 tbsp curry powder
- 1/2 cup dashi broth
- 1 tbsp soy sauce
- 1 tbsp mirin
- 1/2 cup sliced onions
- 1/2 cup sliced carrots
- 1/2 cup cooked chicken or pork (optional)

Instructions:

1. Cook udon noodles according to package instructions and set aside.
2. In a pot, sauté onions and carrots until soft.
3. Add curry powder, dashi broth, soy sauce, and mirin. Simmer for 5 minutes.
4. Add cooked chicken or pork if using and simmer for an additional 5 minutes.
5. Pour the curry sauce over the udon noodles and serve hot.

Rice Ball Trio (Plum, Salmon, Kombu)

Ingredients:

- 2 cups steamed rice
- 1 tbsp umeboshi (pickled plum), chopped
- 1/4 cup cooked salmon, flaked
- 1 tbsp kombu (seaweed), chopped
- Salt, to taste

Instructions:

1. Divide the steamed rice into three portions.
2. For the plum rice ball, mix chopped umeboshi into one portion of rice and form into a ball.
3. For the salmon rice ball, mix flaked salmon into another portion of rice and form into a ball.
4. For the kombu rice ball, mix chopped kombu into the last portion of rice and form into a ball.
5. Lightly salt the rice balls and serve.

Tokyo Milk Tea Pudding

Ingredients:

- 1 1/2 cups whole milk
- 1/2 cup heavy cream
- 2 tbsp loose-leaf black tea (or 2 tea bags)
- 1/4 cup sugar
- 2 eggs
- 1 tsp vanilla extract
- Tapioca pearls (optional)

Instructions:

1. Heat milk and cream in a pot until hot but not boiling. Add the tea leaves and steep for 5 minutes.
2. Strain out the tea leaves and return the liquid to the pot. Add sugar and whisk until dissolved.
3. In a bowl, whisk eggs and vanilla extract. Slowly pour the hot milk mixture into the eggs, whisking constantly to avoid curdling.
4. Return the custard mixture to the pot and cook over low heat until thickened.
5. Pour into cups and refrigerate for at least 2 hours to set.
6. Top with tapioca pearls before serving, if desired.